Michael Jackson;

The allegations by wade robson and James Safechuck and others are they true or false? Is Michael Jackson an innocent victim or a serial pedophile?

Michael Jackson

A. Is Michael Jackson a child predator?
B. IS Wade robson and others are lying
C. My final answer ,final opinion on this tragedy

A.Is Michael Jackson a child predator?

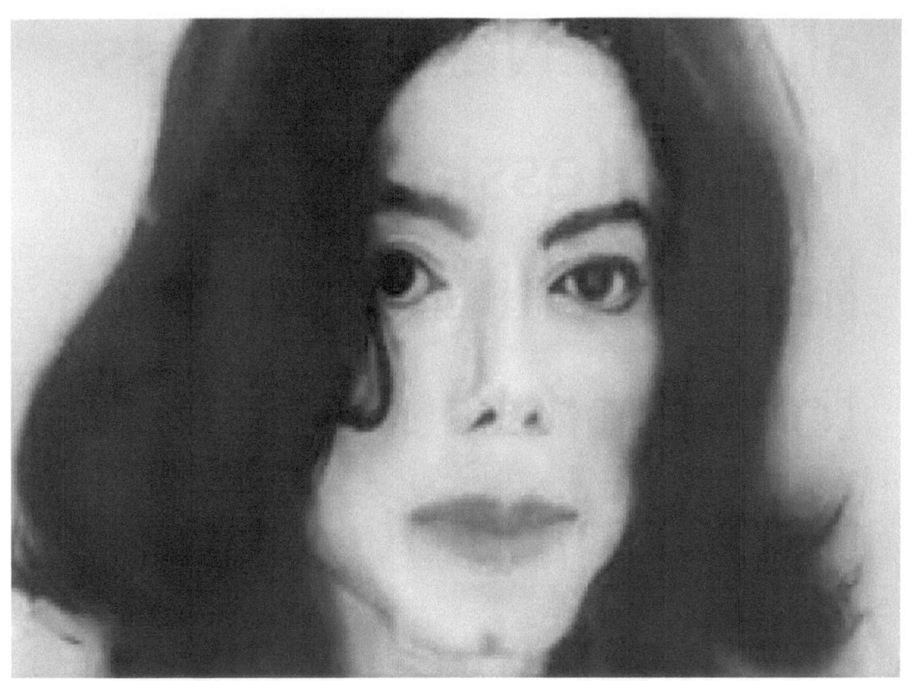

Michael Jackson was and still is one of the biggest music stars of all time. Nevertheless his confession that he had no childhood due to the pressures of performing at young age likely,led to his downfall and death of prescription drug abuse and child molestation allegations but does his lack of childhood,and lack of awareness of reality due to not living a normal life led to him being a child predator,well lets look at the facts

B, Is Jordan chandler and other accusers are lying ?

Wade Robson

1993, Jordan chandler accused him of being a child molester , facts courtesy of several sources

Coutrsey of sources-----On August 18, 1993 the Los Angeles Police Department's Sexually Exploited Child Unit began a criminal investigation into Jackson. The same day, June told police that she did not believe Jackson had molested her son.[11][24] On August 21, a search warrant was issued, allowing police to search Neverland Ranch. Police questioned 30 children who were friends of Jackson, who all stated that Jackson was not a child molester.[10][24] A police officer involved in the investigation told *The Los Angeles Times* that no evidence (medical, photographic or video) could be found that would support a criminal filing.[24]

On the day the allegations were made public, August 24, Jackson began the third leg of his Dangerous World Tour, in Bangkok. That same day, Jackson's investigator held a press conference accusing Chandler of trying to extort $20 million. He did not mention that Jackson had made several counter-offers.[10][24] On August 25, Jackson's young friends Brett Barnes and Wade Robson held a press conference in which they stated that they had slept in the same bed as Jackson, but nothing sexual in nature had occurred.[25][26]Jackson's family held another press conference, saying it was their "unequivocal belief" that Michael was a victim of an attempt to take advantage of his fame and wealth.[25][26]

Jordan chandler's family was asking for money before there was a criminal investigation. Bret Barnes and Wade robson testified that nothing happened between him and Michael Jackson, If you want to look for this source, go to Wikipedia, and google and look it up and make your own decisions. Jordan chandler stated that he can describe Michael jackson's penis. Some of it was corroborated but there was reports that some of what Jordy testify was not corrobatedleading me to believe that there is doubt in this case.

Despite the out of court settlement. The case ended because it was reported that Jordy chandler did not cooperate with the investigation and the grand jurors felt that there were no

damaging evidence against Jackson

Courtesy of sources,,internet

Jackson had revealed in a televised interview that he had vitiligo, a skin disorder that destroys skin pigmentation and creates blotches, and that he used make-up to even out his skin.[60] The interview was watched by 90 million, and after it aired, expert information on vitiligo was widely shared in the media.[60] According to private investigator Anthony Pellicano, who questioned Jordan in July 1993 after hearing Evan's taped phone call, Jordan denied that he ever saw Jackson's body but said he did lift his shirt once to show him the blotches on his skin.[6] Investigators made a probe into Jackson's history, including family interviews, to see if he had undergone procedures to alter his body's appearance, as the grand jury felt there was no clear match with Jordan's description.

Michael Jackson's lifestyle of sleeping with children in his

bedroom give reason to be suspicious of alleged child abuse. Nevertheless,Michael Jackson was someone who was out of touch with reality due to the lack of a normal life since he was a child,and the prescription drugs he taken. Michael Jackson was someone who was taken advantage of because of his fame, at the same time ,he was incapable of understanding the world around him realistically.

The Gavin Arizo investigation 2004-2005

Courtesy of sources

n August 2000, Gavin Arvizo, a boy with cancer in remission, visited Neverland Ranch with his family.[6] Jackson said he invited sick children to his home to have fun because he felt sorry for them; he felt he had been robbed of his own childhood.[7]

In 2003, ITV broadcast a documentary, *Living with Michael Jackson*, for which journalist Martin Bashir interviewed Jackson over eight months.[8] The *Guardian* described the documentary as "the fuse that ignited the case and the trial".[9] In the documentary, Jackson and Arvizo held hands and discussed sleepovers,[2] and Jackson said he had slept in bed with many children. He said: "It's not sexual, we're going to sleep. I tuck them in... It's very charming, it's very sweet."[8] Jackson received criticism and some newspapers called for his children to be removed from his custody.[8] In a press release in February 2003, Sneddon stated that under California law an adult sleeping in bed with a child was not a criminal offense unless "affirmative, offensive conduct" occurs.[

n June 2003, Sneddon reopened the investigation into Jackson.[2] The investigation lasted two years and produced 1,900 pages of grand jury testimony.[11] In August, authorities interviewed Gavin Arvizo, his mother Janet, and younger brother Star.[2] In November, Gavin told police that Jackson had molested him several times in February and March 2003, when, according to Janet, Jackson had held the family captive at Neverland Ranch.[2]

Gavin Arvizo was 15 when he testified.[15] He claimed that, after *Living with Michael Jackson* aired, Jackson had begun serving him and his younger brother wine and making sexual advances.[32] He said that Jackson had masturbated him to ejaculation after they drank alcohol,[33] and then told him that if men do not masturbate, they "might rape a girl".[34] Challenged by Mesereau, who said that Gavin had told sheriffs that his grandmother had said this, Gavin said "I'm not exactly sure what my grandmother told me".[34] Gavin admitted that he had told his school administrator that Jackson had not molested him.[34]

The prosecution alleged that Jackson had exposed Gavin to pornography. Fingerprints from Gavin and Jackson were found on pornographic magazines belonging to Jackson. Mesereau countered that Jackson had caught Gavin reading them and locked them in a briefcase.[23]

The trial heard that Gavin's father had persistently begged celebrities for money after Gavin had been diagnosed with cancer

Macaulay Culkin[edit]

Former child star Macaulay Culkin (pictured in 1991) testified that he had shared a bed with Jackson but had never been abused.

Former child star Macaulay Culkin testified that he had shared a bed with Jackson on a dozen or more times between the ages of 9 and 14, but had never been molested and had never seen Jackson act improperly. He said that his parents had known he was in Jackson's bedroom and "never saw it as an issue".[39] He described shock at hearing the allegations that Jackson had molested him, and dismissed them as "absolutely ridiculous".[39] Culkin said they had bonded over their shared experience of child stardom.[39]

Wade Robson

Wade Robson was five years old when he met Jackson. He testified that he had slept in Jackson's bedroom several times but had never been molested, despite the claims of some witnesses.[40] Years after the trial, Robson changed his position, saying Jackson had abused him.[40]

The jury deliberated for about 32 hours over seven days.[43] On the initial vote, nine jurors voted to acquit Jackson, while three voted that he was guilty.[44] On June 14, 2005, they returned a verdict of not guilty on all charges.[43] Years later, one juror said his "gut feeling" was that Jackson had molested children, but supported the not-guilty decision as he felt that the prosecution had not proved this beyond reasonable doubt.[43]

In 2013,[17] Robson claimed that Jackson had sexually abused him, on two visits to the US and after he moved with his family to the US, when Robson was aged between seven and 14.[18] Robson said his earlier denial was due to Jackson's "complete manipulation and brainwashing", and said that Jackson had said they would both go to jail if anyone learned of the abuse.[17] Robson said that his change of story was provoked by becoming a father and experiencing nervous breakdowns in 2011 and 2012.[21]

In 2015, Robson's case was dismissed by a Los Angeles judge, ruling that Robson had missed the 12-month statutory deadline after Jackson's death.[18] The judge did not rule on the credibility of the allegations.[18] The allegations by Robson and another man, James Safechuck, are the focus of the 2019 documentary *Leaving Neverland*.[18]

Wade robson repeatedly testify that nothing happened between him and Michael Jackson. He stated on television and interviews after Jackson's death in 2009 , that nothing happened . In 2012, Wade Robson reportedly suffer breakdownsand changed his mind that nothing happened.

The truth is , Gavin arizo trial , ; Michael Jackson was found not guilty, Wade robson testified that nothing had happened, Latoya Jackson claimed that Michael Jackson was a pedophile but retracted her story because she claimed that her ex husband influenced her to say bad things about her brother

Facts relating to Latoya Jackson-

Courtesy of facts December 1993, Gordon hastily arranged a press conference in Tel Aviv, where he had Jackson read a statement claiming to believe the sex abuse allegation against her younger brother Michael might be true.[37][38] This was an abrupt reversal of her previous defense of Michael against the charges.[39] Gordon claimed La Toya had proof which she was prepared to disclose for a fee of $500,000. A bidding war between US and UK tabloids began, but fell through when they realized that her revelations were not what she had claimed them to be.[40] According to La Toya, Gordon threatened to have siblings Michael and Janet killed if she didn't follow his orders.[35][41] In 1993, Jackson claims her father Joe Jackson sexually abused her as a child.[42 Jackson was free to speak more openly about the control he exerted over her life. She sent a security expert to eyewitness that Gordon had not faked his death a second time.[52] In 2005 she appeared on ABC News to recant her previous allegations and defend brother Michael against new charges of child abuse.[21] VH1 described Jackson as a role model having weathered various successes and setbacks.[49]

LA toya Jackson

The number of witnesses to the Michael Jackson alleged crimes retracted their statements including Wade robson and safechuck which shows a doubt on what is true and what is not;

Safechuck- courtesy of news

Safechuck and Wade Robson, who's also accused Jackson of child sexual abuse, recognized that viewers may be skeptical of their claims. Both men testified on Jackson's behalf in 1993, after another child, Jordan Chandler, accused the singer of molestation. Despite the backlash, Safechuck and Robson, who are both now married with their own children, said they felt they needed to come forward not to regain favorability in the public eye, but to help others and heal themselves. Safechuck also made it clear that he in no way wants others to feel pressured to share their personal experiences.

James Safechuck- a victim or a liar!

Tarnished Reputation !

No matter what the verdict is or who is telling the truth, Michael Jackson was tarnished ,perhaps forever by allegations that have not proven ,and despite these accusers lack of consistency in their statements or their admission of lying about the allegations. I personally do not know what the truth is .

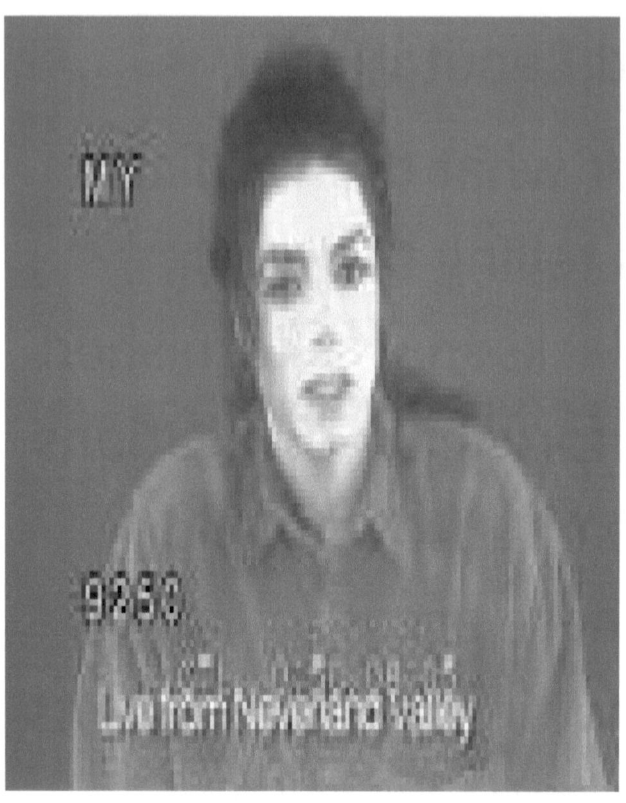

Michael Jackson addressed his innocence of the child molestation allegations in 1993

B, the tabloids, like hard copy and Diane Dimond, helped destroy Michael jackson's image in 1993 by paying ex-employees and others thousands of dollars for claims which show that they were not trustworthy in their claims.

D. My final answer ,final opinion on this tragedy

I am in the defense of neutrality but I see a continuance of reasonable doubt due to the inconsistencies by the two accusers in the HBO documentary “leaving Neverland”and the previous accusers. Money is a likely motivation for the allegations however I do see Michael Jackson as a person who could have committed child abuse and gotten away with it legally but not in the world of public opinion. The truth is that people should not make a decision because the doubt ,and the inconsistences on one side and the questionable behavior of Jackson when he sleeps with children on the other shows that there should be an innocence until proven guilty motto as the right decision . This is especially true now that Jackson is deceased and there was no guilty verdict or smoking gun to prove him molested children beyond a reasonable doubt .

www.ingramcontent.com/pod-product-compliance
Ingram Content Group UK Ltd.
Pitfield, Milton Keynes, MK11 3LW, UK
UKHW041901190726
13854UKWH00003B/1023

9 780359 517206